THE ORPHAN
BEAR

POEMS

Bill Rewak

WILLIAM J. REWAK

ISBN: 1495382168
ISBN 13: 9781495382161

Library of Congress Control Number: 2014902105

CreateSpace Independent Publishing Platform
North Charleston, South Carolina

This book is dedicated, with love, to my siblings
and their spouses, for all of our fun together:

Dana Cole

Patricia and Frank Lima

Robert and Susan Rewak

Michael (in memoriam) and Susan Rewak

CONTENTS

PROLOGUE   xiii
Le Morte d'Arthur   xv

PART I

Choose Any Word   3
Paraphernalia   4
Gaiety   5
White Swans   6
English 400   8
Why I'm Here   9
A New Task   11
Fits And Starts   12
At The Barber's   14
The Ragpicker   15
Roly-Poly   16

PART II

The Play   19
Genesis   20
Primitivism   21
The Orphan Bear   22
As If   24
The Gift   25
Chris Ranes (1929-2002)   27
Silence   28
Good Taste   30
This Moment   32
Joseph   33

PART III

Dick Tracy's World   36

Poppies   37

History   38

The Kneelers   39

The Shivering   41

A Formic Study   42

Roses   44

Parades   46

"Be Still And Wait For The Lord"   47

Boston, April 15, 2013   48

What Were You Like, Really?   50

PART IV

Jumpers   52

The Maker   53

Adam   54

Since You Know   56

Choose The Owl   57

Buttons   59

The Old Chair   60

The Barnyard   61

Form   62

Fine Wine   63

PART V

St. George   67

Angels' Work   68

Remembering El Salvador Jesuit Martyrs Of November 16, 1989 69

A Fitting   71

My Uncle   72

You Alone   74

Heroes   75

A Round Man   76
The Font   78
Ansel Adams (1902-1984)   80
She Stands   81

PART VI

If I Should Die   85
The Terrible Point   87
Hamlet: A Revenge Tragedy   89
Eyesight   90
Transfiguration   91
Jolly Green Giant   92
The Walker   94
Seasoning   95
Passage   96
A Filament of Love   98
Eucharist at Emmaus   99

EPILOGUE   101
These Old Hands   103
ACKNOWLEDGMENTS   107

PROLOGUE

LE MORTE D'ARTHUR

In the middle of the lake,
an arm, clothed in white
samite, holds Excalibur.

When I was ten,
I wanted to ask,
"Didn't the white samite

get wet?" But
I was wise; you never
inquired about the obvious.

Or maybe I guessed —
pierced the teacher's
superior demeanor —

that Art and Reality
are two spinsters
having a feud.

At a simmering fifteen,
the sparkling white samite
moved in sinuous folds

and fell caressingly
on thighs that lay ready
in an imaginary tower.

At a post-graduate twenty-five,
and after Jessie Weston,
the mind clicked off,

in professional understatement,
each symbolic gesture,
each hyacinth girl:

the white samite
was key to the quest
and pointed to pale sorrow.

In England at thirty-five,
an adventurous skepticism
roamed Tintagel,

made the pilgrimage
to Glastonbury Tor
and squinted at the grave.

Now, at my mellow end,
Mallory's dream
has entered my blood:

the white samite
tells my pain
and orders my world.

PART I

HOPE'S SUN IS SEEN OF EVERY EYE:
THE HALO THAT IT GIVES
IN NATURE'S WIDE AND COMMON SKY
CHEERS EVERYTHING THAT LIVES.

John Clare, "Emmonsales Heath"

CHOOSE ANY WORD

I'll just put a word down here,
it's called "word," and it expands

or shrinks depending on how much air
we blow into it: daintily perfumed air,

not your bag of winds, for it must
be palatable to refined tastes

and accessible to downhome personnel;
a word must jump and dance,

fit around a Virginia reel or a minuet,
it must know when to slide and when

to turn and block all opponents;
its richness depends on where

it was born and how it clothed itself
as it grew into its peculiar power,

its wisdom depends on how often
it has traveled; but above all, its life

depends on those who value its beauty.

PARAPHERNALIA

What do we get from all the connectedness
we've devised? My iPhone speaks to my iPad

which gurgles into my desktop and eventually
flashes onto my TV. What we do with wireless

we have done until now with sly looks, vocal chords,
flesh-on-flesh, even a kick in the butt; all of this,

however, has been digitalized to fit a more
convenient space; it's been diagrammatically

arranged for easier access, more effective control.
Circles have become squares, cloudbursts deleted,

I sit up straight rather than slouch, have forgotten
how to preface gracefully or conclude with a coda.

What do I get? I have become a shadow, a mite;
but if you threaten my paraphernalia, I can still bite.

GAIETY

After years of digging
I've turned up a little clown
    in my soul:
wild red grin
and astonished eyes,
a halo of blond,
a soupçon of irony
    in the blood,
and I present him
to the world
    and to myself,
hoping that any dark miasma
I've become encased in
may thaw and run back
into the earth to be cleansed
and I'll form
    a gospel
for other lonely diggers
who will also discover,
when they have grown brittle,
that there is a layer of gaiety
    hidden
that takes only a morning's
song of wonder
to reveal its bristling life.

WHITE SWANS

Pause now
and watch:

the sun's ready
to shine, to drop

sparkles, ignite
each house

with early dawn
with the song

of larks rising,
wait and see

if such a song
can burrow

into my heart
strip the old

shackles and reveal
a moment, clear

and just, pure
as the white swans

of Stratford, agile
as a wing aloft,

so I'm ready to greet
the day You've set

aside for me.

ENGLISH 400

She bounces in from McDonald's
where she serves time
    each day
and offers her latest take:
she is particularly rife
with symbols, likes to throw one
    in every paragraph
to ensure the professor is paying close
attention:
a rainbow in this one,
a hawk in one farther on
a pitchfork
in the extra one over here
(he'll never get that)
but they are all jumbled
    in a pile
without proper periods
    or commas
and the conjunctions
just don't work
because some symbols are inferior
    to others
and need a dependent position
but she is convinced her world
    rumbles on
in an all-embracing exegesis
    of desire
and cannot be concerned
with nuts and bolts.

WHY I'M HERE

I'm waiting for this appointment, you see,
because last night as the stars looped
outside my window and beckoned me
to join their games, I felt intimidated
and knew I could not measure up — light
cannot find an entry into my heart —
so I turned aside to watch the wallpaper
grow. That was boring and I realized
serious steps had to be taken; that's why
I'm here. Well, this morning, too,
when the New York Times didn't arrive,
but on the doorstep I found only a squirrel
looking up at me with a smile of anticipation,
I figured there was more going on
than I could reasonably handle alone,
so here I am. Oh, and my taxi ride here:
he insisted on driving past three
cemeteries because he divined I've built
a life on death, yes, I think it important
we lay orchids carefully on graves
to indicate beauty has been suspended
for a time, but that may not be why
I'm here; although when I was riding up
in the elevator, I could hear planets
move, and weeds were making a hell
of a noise (flowers don't make noise),
and though that happens rarely,
it may be worth a conversation or two.
When I walked in, your eyes were spinning —

they reminded me of the celestial rhythms
we were once so fond of — and when you said
I had to wait a bit, I was pleased because
I wanted to gather my ideas and render
them much more logical than perhaps
I've so far described them, but I tend to bare
all these experiences more candidly
than is proper so I apologize if I've embarrassed
you or taken advantage of your time:
your hands are so beautifully alive there,
held aloft over the computer keys as if
in amazement at what they are about to discover
but are waiting, too, for some surcease -
and the vision I now have of your place
in the universe may also be why I'm here.

A NEW TASK

(In Memory of Gerard Manley Hopkins, S.J.)

Do you, in your wild willful love, wander
through places you'd always longed for,

soft-step through forests of words
you glean like bursting mushrooms;

do you learn the trails and leave a leaf,
red with the rust of autumn, here and there,

to map your returns; have you discovered
the land your Greek verbs sang so sweetly of,

your Welsh nouns placed in woods and vales?
Do you see, finally, after the dimness

that shadowed your black-robed walks
down lanes of half-opened eyes,

all the sentences left to be completed?
Is your pen busy with new, full-blown

wonders - stanzas that startle the saints?
Startle them! Pleasure them with sound!

Even saints can learn a new language.

FITS AND STARTS

I get up at 4 am
then nod off to sleep
3 or 4 times
during the day
and go to bed
at 11 so I'm always
tired; it's very like
squinching on prayer
and then sprinkling
words around
the day but finding
a yawning hole
in the heart
or reading in fits
and starts
then missing the plot.
We bump through life
hitting potholes
and scraping bushes
so the new car
that was supposed
to provide a soft,
focused ride
winds up
an old jalopy
that coughs and spits

a Neanderthal
whose windows
are fogged
whose doors
never open now.
Have to find
a good wrench,
a softer pillow,
a book that will set
my toes ablaze,
and a direct line to You.

AT THE BARBER'S

I went to the barber's
this afternoon
to have him fix my hair
because he botched it
last Tuesday
he had cut a little here
and thinned a bit there
and I came away looking like
a frightened magpie
so I returned and had him edit
while I sat
watching the Kentucky Derby
I thought
it would be nice to have someone
edit my soul this way
cut a bulge here
smooth the curl there
and I'd come away
with a smooth-textured look
I could present at judgment
I'd run my own race
I'd say:
it's not winning or losing (sure!)
it's the slant on the bend
the careful stretch of the neck
the white kernel of fairness
without cutbacks or side swipes
when the hair is smooth
the race is clean
and the soul sits back, content.

THE RAGPICKER

I don't think about you

though I know you're heading this way

covered in cast-offs, down the stony hill
you pull your cart, a treasure trove
filled with leavings: a child's sailor suit,
a red flowing wig, a velvet cape
that skirted floors in palaces, two canes,
an emerald earring in the pocket
of a gentleman's vest, and some worn,
bloodied trousers

you've raked them from lives
from vessels that no longer had need
and now you trundle into my village
and knock on my door to measure
my coat, wipe my shoes

and I wonder, where were you born, ragpicker,
what ancient covenant gave you the right
to harvest?

ROLY-POLY

He was a roly-poly, loved sitting on camels
because they swayed and in his heart
he was both dancer and adventurer, looking
beyond the tight folds of his tent,

so he was eager to join their fanciful journey
despite the brigands along the way:
"I'll sit on them!" he said. The others huffed
but needed his sense of direction, so off

they went, four black swans gliding
across the sand; conversation was hesitant
because they did not know what they'd find
and wondered in the blue evenings if they'd

have to change their ways: roly-poly was eager
but he'd not want to diet; the others felt
an unknowable need to explore, but feared
their find as they would a god's displeasure;

they crested a hill, silhouetted against the moon,
then swatted the camels and rode into the valley,
determined to see it through: the star shone
on a stable: they paused, and alighted.

Imagination does not take the step inside:
it would intrude on an encounter we cannot
decipher, where wise men put on new robes
and roly-poly discovered why he was happy.

PART II

O STRUGGLING WITH THE DARKNESS
ALL THE NIGHT,
AND VISITED ALL NIGHT BY
TROOPS OF STARS.

Samuel Taylor Coleridge,
"Hymn before Sunrise,
In the Vale of Chamouni"

THE PLAY

You come to an almost-end
and wonder if at any point
along the way you've hit
the mark, if the chalk lines
they've inscribed for you

have been followed; you
fear there were digressions
not planned for in rehearsal
and you may have even left
the stage for another play

or worked in the night
on a bare platform with no help
from your co-stars and ad-libbed
unnecessarily; but, after all,
some imagination had to come

into play, otherwise we squawk
like parrots and roam green
fields with no Falstaff as guide;
the aching question is whether
our imagination betrays us,

leads us to where home,
at last, will be lost,
or if it is a parallel web
of chalk lines meant to bolster
the original play.

GENESIS

A soul fell
into darkness
where it met monsters
it had never seen before

and though it stretched
toward a star
    far off
in a space it yearned for

it stumbled on rocks
and harvested twigs
that had been cast
aside

all the longing
it felt seemed
    deception

but it knew darkness
was a place for learning

that if life
were to spring
it would begin here.

PRIMITIVISM

Oedipus may have started the whole thing
but for him it wasn't the dark underside
of a complicated neurosis.
It was first a disagreement at the Cleft Way
and then a hungry sphinx who wanted to play
beside the high walls of Thebes;
after the riddle was prudently deciphered
he paraded his swollen feet
before the adulation of a crowd
and knelt to the blind glitter of a crown.
Finally, of course, it was a matter
of baby blue eyes
and a penchant for older women.

(For my fellow Greek class members, 1954)

THE ORPHAN BEAR

One evening as clouds of doubt pressed more boldly
than before, a bear with a bouquet of daffodils knocked

on my door. I thought: I should suspect door-ringing bears —
ought they not to be more blunt? But the bear's politeness

threw me off, and I agreed. He ponderously lay, an ancient
rug in front of my fireplace, and then slept, this orphan bear

whose rheumy eyes dreamed inward on a world of dark forests,
giant ferns and wide, pink streams. What would he turn into,

I wondered. This had to be a grim joke, this lump of primitive
muscle smiling silently in a living room in suburbia.

At the stroke of midnight, he stirred - but remained covered with fur.
He spoke softly then about the burdens of his mission,

his love for God, his troublesome back. I thought, why
confine myself to stray dogs - so I offered him my home,

my prayers, my own love. He nodded gratefully and placed
his great bear paw on my head. But, he said, he had a journey

to complete — and a touch of wizardry rumbled in his throat
as he sought to explain the years he'd yet to see. His wizardry

was comfort: he soothed the mourning fever that grew inside me
and eased the hollow wind that drops neither leaves nor rain,

for I had only painted clowns on bright walls; I needed his wisdom to enchant, to dig further and etch a deeper vein.

But in the soft of night, he picked up his bouquet of daffodils, bowed his head, and lumbered out the door.

Under the street lamp, he turned. "I will miss you," I called. And I do.

AS IF

Two empty lawn chairs
on the edge of the bluff
sit facing one another

as if two friends had finished
their Jack Daniels, rose
in laughter and moved in

to a more somber evening
by firelight; or as if two lovers
decided they should leave

the chairs that way to mark
the moment of their parting;
as if two nuns had stopped

their rosary on a sudden
to run for the child left
by the roadside; as if

moved there by the gardener
who could not foresee the anguish
such a sight would cause.

THE GIFT

How did we last, through all the years,
how did we last through ten-cent movies,

beehives, blackberries, midnight
forests, how did we know we were safe?

When I fell out of a plum tree,
not able to speak, the breath in me

fighting to come alive, how did I know
she'd be there, holding, pressing me

against breasts of comfort, how
did I know that storms could rage

and ice could cover our little place,
the wind could spell its fury, but I'd know

her hand: did I learn that through the birth
canal, and did I extend my lesson

to those who came after, to the ones
I cherish because we all have her blood?

We have all searched the papers
that delineate time and place,

but they are numbers, not strength
and purpose, not the carnal desire

we were born from, and not her daily routine
that limned our spirit - and something

beyond that, a confession of heartache
a begging for a spark that would ignite

our skin and leave us breathless.

CHRIS RANES (1929-2002)

A child walks fire in the streets of Warsaw
(wearing tweed nubbed with green
but honored by a smear of red);

she blossoms amid faces torn by death,
grows muscle in elbowing the SS.
We ask:

from that seed grows art?
A wondrous alembic she carries:
the process goes back, beyond time,

where water, earth, fire and air
squeeze out form from emotion stripped
and hope grasped, from love offered

in pain,
from a flaming ghetto and betrayal,
from safe nights in star-filled forests.

All burst into streaks of color
that fill canvases with news. What you have left
will light our world and forever harbor peace.

SILENCE

I'm holding your hand -
so little else to hold onto

the years have slipped
and leave silver dust behind

memories walk away
in multi-colored coats
all strong hues
leave their mark

a door opens and closes
with white efficiency

but you're silent

and I try to be also
because once there were
so many words
they confused the day

here there is no confusion
only a bed and a chair

and perhaps because
striding across a room
you were always
larger than the rest
an extra pillow
to lay away the hours

while we wait.

GOOD TASTE

I have a son, two years old, whose boldness is unrivaled: he has determined to take advantage of my ample library. I would not object, in reasonable circumstances, to his sampling each book, savoring each poem, letting the words roll deliciously over his tongue, for I've encouraged his literary freedom and showed him delectable pictures, read him stories of gourmet quality. In my world, children should be taught good taste.

But I walked in recently to peruse Hazlitt and found my son eating him. My book lay in tatters. Half the immortal words were digesting, mortally, in the stomach of a boy who had learned to love the classics. Since then, I have buried the Wife of Bath and her fellow pilgrims, Othello, a white whale, and a generous portion of Walt Whitman. Unable to break his appetite, I have tried to encourage a taste for Kingsley, Butler, and Beattie, but his education has been too successful: he scorns the appetizers and prefers strong meat. And in company, he amazes: he hiccups in iambic pentameters and sneezes in couplets; he belches in breathtaking stentorian indignation. At night, his dreams rumble in an uncertain rhythm – with just a note of classical cadence. (He has become, in so short a time, a perspicacious critic of my every word: the lines he eats I mourn for; the lines he leaves I sweep away with yesterday's dust.)

What does one do with a son who devours libraries: hire him out as an editor? (The publishing world would thrive for he'd eat the gold and leave the dross for profit.) Book him for poetry readings? (Every poem is tucked inside, ready to be disgorged.) Put him to teach? (He'd frighten students who are used to a more genteel literary criticism.)

But sometimes, now, I notice he walks into the library with sadness – is it the tragedy in his bowels, or his own ingested perception that perfection of line has never been achieved and that his hunger will forever haunt him?

My second son will be educated in a sandbox.

(For Don Dodson)

THIS MOMENT

This moment
when You
are here
is all I ask,
just a small
slice of time;
I will plant it
water it
with seconds
left over
from the cutting
nurture it
with hours
I've tucked away
saved for just
this planting,
step aside
and watch
my small time
grow into
a new life
with the lilt
of the past
the dance of now
the grace
of what's to come.

JOSEPH

You didn't mind
when he went about
his Father's business

a puzzle, of course,
for he was your son, too,
and you loved him

you showed him
edges on the wood
and how it would curl

you fashioned the joinings
so two dimensions
made three, you gave him

the tools to build
but the home he built
stands on Golgotha

you could not know
how he would use
your gift.

PART III

ERE THE PARTING HOUR GO BY,
QUICK, THY TABLETS, MEMORY!

Matthew Arnold, "A Memory Picture"

DICK TRACY'S WORLD

Do you recall the inventive criminals
who wandered Dick Tracy's world? Ugly
and aggressive, Dick was right to best them;

if Cueball or Gruesome were to step
onto our sidewalks, they'd fright us all;
they juggled goodness like a glass toy.

During the day, they were safe on a page:
I'd walk with them, their horror contained
in a small colored strip I held in my hand.

But in the evening as I lay in sleep,
I let them out and allowed their play;
they took over and I was one of them,

belying every code I had learned;
dreams were the cloak I used as I told
myself their company was preferable.

POPPIES

Nowhere else do poppies spring
so lightly to the surface of the mind
than here on this strange planet
that flew off as a piece of earth
some twenty million years ago:
it spun, gyrated, gamboled
into the sharp tail of our Milky Way
and settled into a place left vacant
by a cold moon in search of warmer
climes. Still holding the music of earth
in its belly, it can move splendidly
to a dirge, but its better dance is now
a wild bolero, winging off sparkles
that become its own new stars.
Fretted to movement by the chill, but eager
to be different, it long ago recognized
that the universe needed a comedian;
thus rivers climb clouds, rocks ripen
into marshmallows and what we beg for
is what we get. Turning far from any sun,
it will last.

HISTORY

When we think of the past, we have to be ruthless,
we have to jettison prejudices and dreams,

all the silver words we thought we heard,
all the dark strokes we may have painted;

that's what I do when I travel to the small space
back there in the tight box of my life

where larks seldom sang, but no ogres
rose from under the bridge, no nightmares

I could not combat; and if a werewolf moved
in the trees I could say it was not there.

I try to get close - knowing that lapses
are inevitable, the river switches course -

in order to see only a moment, hold it carefully,
whisk away the dust and hope it will shine.

If that can be done once, then a second time
is possible, and perhaps these stairs eventually

will form a ladder and I'll be able to climb
to a clean history, a portrait with the brush of truth.

(For Nelle Harper Lee)

THE KNEELERS

The old retainer, bent now,
dusts the top of the altar
every morning at nine,
kneels to brush the cobwebs,
then drinks what's left of the wine:
no one notices because prayer
captures all their attention.
They're searching the "wine of life,"
they say, and return to their knees.
He has knelt too many years
to expect spiritual enlightenment
on the floor, but doesn't begrudge them;
his knees were always less nimble.
At twelve he serves the stew
then adds a drop of claret,
for himself, to enliven the carrots;
from four to six he cleans
the living quarters, chasing mice
from under the beds and sweeping
away sweet memories,
while testing the Abbot's brandy;
at eight he kneels in the kitchen
to clean the lower cupboard
where the Sunday sauterne is kept,
then allows himself a joyous dance
in the garden's soft moonlight,
mimicking David before the Ark;
at nine he's back at the altar

preparing bread and wine
for the morning's ritual.
He's refused lighter positions,
insisting that kneeling is invigorating,
that the monks could not survive
without his solicitude for the details
and left-overs of life.
He's the quiet presence that makes
their isolation possible, and he is aware
that daily and adequate compensations
come in many ways.

THE SHIVERING

It was a shivering day
icicles stuck in the heart of noon
we walked through soft white
down to the shore
to watch tankers plow
through waves to deliver
their coal.

Childhood is a puzzle
of memories: hard to fit the pieces
so they mirror the whole.

Seasons melt into one another:
ice and sun may not be
the true shapes; their glaze
is tricky: the shivering
may be only yesterday's pain.

But there is no loss:
the jumble is a treasure to be sorted
at leisure.

A FORMIC STUDY

An ant crawled in here last night
and stopped on the edge of my desk
(I was going to say "sat" but though I'm sure he did
it was hard to tell); his graceful feelers
swiveled and swerved, testing the right
words to declaim his indignation. He spoke,
at first, in accents Chaucerian - I sensed
a primordial de-bump, de-bump and marked
a penchant for courteous allegory - but then
changed to the chittering of a pious Pound.
Was not this inconsistent with his presumably myopic
view of life? How did the ant kingdom
produce such a prodigy?

He told me,
sniffing there on the edge of my desk,
"You think because I'm small and brief
I cannot challenge the rhythm of the stars?
You think because I break apart with ease
I cannot see the reasons whole? You think
because I eat your crumbs I turn aside
your diamonds? And you think because I run in trails
I do not search your God? In the desert, when time
began, my sure-footed ancestors outjumped yours,
but a new impulse fused and led you
past your betters. Our mission now
is to wait."

He twitched one feeler
and winked the opposite eye. Since then,
I've noticed he's had a line of visitors
who each hour gather to read, and to pray.

ROSES

I was dreaming this afternoon
in the rose garden behind the shed,

hoeing and snipping, dispensing water,
watching the light move slowly:

twelve bushes, a reasonable variety
of flame petals, a white, a bright

Shakespearean pink. A small space
for such liberality.

Standing in the middle, my heel fell
deeper than such ground should allow.

Puzzled, I pressed with some exertion
and all gave way.

This I discovered: a hole.
Not just a hole.

A great hole under the bushes
where roots jigsawed in and around

one another's private space -
which made me wonder:

Which roots belonged to which bush?
Had some dark grafting been going on

in silence? An upside-down, thieving
world in there and I was not told.

Tonight, when I pray in shadows,
I must ask God about roses.

PARADES

You should look out your window every morning
and then imagine a parade of clowns, of Canterbury

pilgrims, scarlet-bedecked horses stepping high,
with little tots running alongside, yelling and waving

flags, a Lord High Mayor in glistening velvet presiding
in a gold chariot pulled by - camels! If you agree

to use your imagination, anyone or anything can float by.
And what is the use of all this, you ask? There's a battery

somewhere near the pituitary gland that electrifies
an inborn theater, and every glance we take sets

in motion a new reel that unwinds in spite of ourselves:
it quickens our senses and like alcohol or cocaine

makes us addicts; we end up reaching in every day
to ensure the battery is still live so we don't miss

a moment of each parade. And what is the use of all this,
you ask? No use, that's the beauty of it.

"BE STILL AND WAIT FOR THE LORD"

(Psalm 46)

Forgive me, Lord, for being mundane
but waiting for You is liking waiting

for the Muse: You're sporadic, fleeting,
and other spirits join in for confusion;

a pure word from You is like a pure line
for my poem, Your absence a blank page,

Your nod like the joy when a period ends
the quest. But yesterday I sat for an hour

looking at my screen when You jumped in;
today I sat for a dry hour with the psalms

when the Muse sneaked in with a line
I immediately jotted down, so I wonder now:

Do we have two railroad tracks or just one?

BOSTON, APRIL 15, 2013

I was intent on running and avoiding
the knock-kneed, grey-headed bumbler
in front of me who was only there
for a lark, breathless though he surely was;
his elbows, like sharp ravens, pecked at me;
his sweat, flung back, stung my eyes.

We were all in the same churning wave
rolling down Boylston Street, for fun, for fame,
for a camera's eye, for showing off the stripped-down
vehicle we had molded for the pleasure of molding,
for the challenge of the finish line and to drink in
the applause that showered us like cool water;

but the grey-headed bumbler was scissoring me,
his legs flailing, amateur muscles jumping
this way and that like a drunk daddy-long-legs;
hemmed in by tanks on either side, I hung back,
took a new breath and watched for the window,
determined I'd show him who was boss.

Then, my ears could not hear, a hard pillow
thumped me in the face and an army of needles
attacked my knees. We wonder, in a split second
sometimes, if what we have gained from life is finally
all loss, if running to keep in front leaves us, at last,
without legs, on a hot, red pavement.

Memory is a puzzle of a thousand pieces
we labor over to fit together the past, but the only piece
I now have in my hand is that of a grey-headed bumbler,
bent over me, his lips moving in words I could not hear,
squeezing my thighs to stop my life from leaving,
and I do not know his name.

WHAT WERE YOU LIKE, REALLY?

What were you like, really?
I know the plot, the parables,
the swine skipping off the cliff;
but in the morning, before the crowds,

when milk and bread were on the table
and the sun was just reaching,
when empty doorways spoke silence,
did you lean back and yawn?

Who wiped the table?
Were your sandals tight?
We watch you move and heal
and we know the power distilled in a tear,

we watch great clouds descend
in a transfiguring light
and all these we parse
with a 2000-year-old history;

but it's the cups and saucers
I want to know
because there your smile is revealed
as the day sets out

as the work begins.

PART IV

AND THIS OUR LIFE, EXEMPT FROM PUBLIC HAUNT,
FINDS TONGUES IN TREES, BOOKS IN RUNNING BROOKS,
SERMONS IN STORIES, AND GOOD IN EVERYTHING.

William Shakespeare, *As You Like It*

JUMPERS

Have you watched them? All the jumpers?
Rabbits, kangaroos, grasshoppers, all those

God has given a special talent of being light
on their feet? They quietly share a secret:

an ability to touch a space others cannot reach,
and they know if they can hold that space,

encircle it, they won't begrudge their big feet.

THE MAKER

I can't sit here staring at a ceramic horse
all afternoon watching the sun move

from snout to rump and not think idly
that its maker must have adored his subject

so lovingly does it curve and swell, so
majestic its intent; how fondly has he

smoothed its neck and taught us tension,
how carefully the lesson expressed

that one must become something other
when one creates, something close

to an afternoon's movement of the sun.

ADAM

"And Love, the human form divine. . . ."
William Blake, *Songs of Innocence*

That first moment I awoke
and my life stepped into time,

I let go the earlier years —
lying lifeless in a no-past -

and began to record
the movement of the sun

to translate my growing limbs;
strange to note how the death

of a rose could help me fit
time and place and how

the birth of a cub could give me
wonder; how great trees mocked

my new days; how marvelous
that she who stood beside me,

whose eyes slowly opened
on a green expanse that flowed

to an horizon we had not known
could so easily show me

how *love* begins.

SINCE YOU KNOW

You're lying there in satin now,
after a few days of hard breath and pale eyes.
You're lying there with a rosary - and psalms
at your elbow. About all you'll need, I suppose.
The uncleanness of the preparation you would have been
jumpy about: you would have handled it more gently -
with a little fuss, maybe, but
gently.

Let me ask you something:
I've looked through all the boxes you collected -
even the smaller ones - and found only tissue.
More than a hundred boxes, stored with fastidious hope.
Was there, finally, nothing to send?
Or were you waiting for something to keep?

I've checked your interrupted pages, vignettes
of forgotten Renaissance princes: you tried
with every word to keep them running, keep them
buying mistresses.

For the time being, I will store them in your boxes,
back in the cramped closet
near a mound of dry straw.

There now, the candles are lit, the music starts,
and we march. But first, my friend - since you know -
is everything suitable?
And shall we continue?

CHOOSE THE OWL

An invitation from squirrels is embarrassing
because their nest is not big enough
for the ideas we bring to dissect; an invitation
from lions is more roomy, but they're inclined
to be impatient with metaphysics and the last thing
you want during an evening of polite conversation
on Aristotle is an angry meat-eater.
Ostriches are afraid of dialogue, chimpanzees
can't keep their minds on track for long,
and the hippopotamus is far too ponderous.
The whale would take our breath away,
and the more obscure they are - the gnu? —
the more difficult to brief on our questions;
nor has the moose even yet studied Heraclitus.
We are often left with the Labrador
who at least is accommodating and wags his tail
in earthy assent. But if you want to know
why mortality reigns or why action
is a consequence of being, choose the owl.
He is attentive to all in the seminar,
swerving his head from one to the other,
blinking seldom and then only
at the outrageous expletives philosophers use
to spice their musings. He asks "How?"
and "Who?" with polite regard for our ignorance
and fashions the graceful air as his pulpit
(but with no dogmatic insistence); a gentleman,
he approaches death kindly, urges
that we look carefully into the flowing stream

and see not only spent leaves
but stolid boulders that purify its journey.
Even the owl, however, cannot see
beyond. So few of these - our friends -
can stay the sting of creation; so few
can forge a bond between the soul and fire.

BUTTONS

The three buttons on my coat sleeve
click when I move, so people turn their

heads and wonder about my sobriety, but I look
them squarely in the eye as if to say I know

very well about my clicks, that music
has always played in and around my skin

and that if this particular brand of music
offends them I will install larger buttons

to remind them of the drums that play inside
us all; but they are intent only on judgment

and cannot fathom the lilt that a bevy of buttons
can give someone who enjoys the consternation.

THE OLD CHAIR

We never walked the same path,
though we tried a few walks together
one year, looking at the sky
and marveling at the distance in space;

we never paced the same room
though we inhabited the same house
and read the same papers on mornings
that never became distinct enough.

We never spoke. A wave across a lawn,
an attempt to explain my day
(a filial privilege compromised by haste) -
these glanced off, dribbled away,

like the words you tried to use
at the end. We never touched,
except in gentlemanly greeting. The wonder
of all is that you are nearer now,

in the back of my car, behind the music
I play, between the words on this page,
than ever you were when you sat, hunched,
in the old chair you loved at home.

THE BARNYARD

So bring them all in, gather the geese,
chickens, the donkey, make room for the cow

even the annoying rooster who hasn't
a good word for anyone, empty the barnyard,

we want all of you to be safe here where
the fire burns warm and we can enjoy

your company; it's not often a guest arrives
so sit quietly while we bathe his feet and mix

the corn; I've heard his glance can turn a head
and make granite blanch; I've heard his touch

can paralyze the underworld, his word can halt
lightning; but do not be intimidated, he wants

only a rest and welcomes your comments
because you, too, have a stake in this endeavor;

you, too, note human folly but have always
remained still: now, speak up and air your

wisdom, let him know he has friends who will
guard his walk, carry him along the lane,

crow when a traitorous word is spoken.
He is happy to receive any help you can give.

FORM

I like the curvature of the lamp
on my desk: wide brim
with thin, embellished neck
and solid pancake base,

a figure from ancient times.
Form is where we came from:
it endures. But give me
light: what form determines

how two hearts spark
interest, how a child grows,
how nations war? What ancient
curvature of the soul set

the die for how we live?
Once the lamp has been formed,
it opens the darkness forever;
once love occurs,

the heart has been torn
forever; once a child
grows strong
and seeks wisdom, others

will follow; once
nations discover power,
war is forever.
Forms endure.

FINE WINE

He felt sometimes he was talking to wood
    to scarecrows
      hay-for-brains
he loved them but they could not imagine
    his plight.
He spent dusty hours on roads of Galilee
words spilled out hour by hour
and they lapped it up thinking it milk
when it was fine wine they had never
    tasted.
At night when moonlight was hesitant
and the waves of Genesaret fell asleep
he'd walk the sand and hold the scent
of evening blossoms
    in his hand
and feel his Father close:
    that healed the wounds.
At daybreak he'd try again
he'd try again with a grain of wheat.

PART V

THERE IS NO LIFE OF A MAN, FAITHFULLY RECORDED, BUT IS A HEROIC POEM OF ITS SORT, RHYMED OR UNRHYMED.

Thomas Carlyle, *Critical and Miscellaneous Essays*

ST. GEORGE

It isn't often I'm invited to meet a visiting poet
so I accepted the invitation even though my soul

was chattering in anticipation and right to my fingertips
I felt a buzz because you can't approach Mt. Parnassus

without knowing you're just a shadow of trees on its flank;
you may strut like a dragon, puffing your blue smoke

in the dusty alleyways of a student's mind, but dragons
are notoriously made of paper and glue, not ready

for a St. George glaring down at the receiving line;
I bungled in and though I felt like I'd dropped my trousers

in the middle of "La Bohème" I greeted him and spoke
of his articulate mastery, his indelible line, his arching music,

not to mention his diaphanous allusions, but the twinkle
in his eyes then turned me honest:"Your poems bring me

joy." He took my arm and we strolled through a garden
of magnolia trees, azaleas and forget-me-nots,

fondling words and leaping over long sentences
until the party noise collapsed and dawn arose;

he thanked me, and as he walked away into the light,
I saw under his cloak the gleam of a silver scabbard.

ANGELS' WORK

We think of them as wistful, cloudy presences,
airy wings protecting our souls from harm,

but Rilke knew the terrifying side, Michael
and his brood, countless Thrones and Dominations,

armies marching on the wind: the insubstantial
giving way to muscle and sword and impossible

beauty; but did he know their secret work:
roaming the universe to keep orbits true,

blocking meteors and pushing infinity
ever outwards, to a point where it enters light

and spills out, cascading stars and nebulae
and space junk into a realm where terror

is no longer needed, immensity is comprehended
like smiles and sweet wine at a dinner table,

where galaxies romp with the gleeful angels
and planets are marbles for their play - and we?

We are allowed front row seats to marvel
at how the universe, if given the chance,

can gather up its riches and kneel for a blessing.

(For John and Rita Carroll)

REMEMBERING EL SALVADOR JESUIT MARTYRS OF NOVEMBER 16, 1989

"These martyrs were killed for the way they lived,
that is, for how they expressed their faith in love."
Dean Brackley, S.J.

I am a garden
Yo soy un jardín
I grow the *Flor de Izote* and *Loroco*
and orchids that blush with morning's light
seeds are deep in me
    they die
and then burst into the colors I love

I am one with every world of spring

I glow in the sunlight
and dance in the breeze
I lie open to what my gardener desires

but seeds are different
and there are different desires:
that morning, early,
eight seeds fell into my soil

there were footsteps and clamoring
the breeze had stilled
so harsh sounds ricocheted
and my dust hung lifeless in the air
my autumn leaves shriveled

I felt the weight of impress
of possible new planting.

Now, I grow stronger
and bloom with a fresh grace
    each year
petals livelier than before
send their scent
out on an eager breeze

to tell the news:

Yo soy un jardín nuevo.

A FITTING

He's looking for a pair of pants,
simple enough, one that will fit

the growing contours of thighs, butt,
and embarrassing waist and it's undressing

and trying and fitting that's tedious
because cloth and contour seldom

match: like trying to fit
the soul into dogma, a laugh

into a new neighborhood
or a Hummer into a 1930's garage -

and how did Noah really fit
all those animals into his boat?

He kneels in the evening and prays
that he will fit into the Kingdom

where the sizes, he is reminded,
range from X Small Pygmy to XXX Large Tall -

that's some consolation.

MY UNCLE

My uncle woke early, shouldered a length
of rope and went out with Rover and Hi Ho to pull

tree stumps out of the ground: Rover barked
encouragement and Hi Ho had to pull, with my uncle

jostling and wrenching and getting his sockets yanked.
The sun inched upward and spread a golden glow

on the early mist: he tried to inhale what he felt
that cold morning, to keep it stored in his lungs

so it could spring out later when he needed it, when the pots
and pans took over; he had never expected to find

treasure on this land, his days wore on as he was told
they would; he had vowed to keep them clean, never

to barter them away and he was regarded as upright, a man
with pressed trousers when necessary and a well-shaven smile.

In the evening, after he scrubbed, he was rewarded with a beer
and newspaper, meat and potatoes. "Love is ever

a stretch," he'd tell me. His eyes had beamed when Hi Ho
brought forth a foal but of late they had darkened often,

even in the bright haying fall when the air felt
sharp. The promises he had made limped along

without foresight, scraggly, in need of brushing. "I need
to wash my lungs," he said, and when he walked the lane

at night he was waiting, I think, not for a dream
as you and I would but for another cold morning

to provide the test he needed for faith.

YOU ALONE

Help me now, Lord,
to say this prayer
so it is not forced
through the eye
of a needle but
has a wide avenue
arched with magnolias:
that You alone
hold this flesh
in Your hand so
it does not flake
that You alone
know the desire
that so often
veers aside
but rights itself
time and again
because You alone
can fill every want
and there is no wall
anymore, just
a small space
I have to cross
so small I can reach
with a whisper of love.

HEROES

I've watched you sitting there
and wonder, do you realize
what heroes are made of?
The grit in your mind that made
you question, the sharp stabs
you made at all of our balloons,
yes, the needles that made us sit
uneasily and your words that spilt
and broke on your plate, all
have been blunted as you sit
watching hummingbirds
whisk by your window, watching
the crocus rise again: these
now are the issues you ponder,
but they are no less significant
than the ones that moved
mountains, they still demand
attention, they demand time
as you sit there wondering
what all the fuss was about.

A ROUND MAN

While I wait to enter the room
where they're all gathered, singing,

I think on why they're there and why
I've been invited: he was a round

man who could squeeze into any hole,
a malleable peg who disdained

dimensions and touted freedom
from rectangular certainty; he rolled

down a hill once to prove obstacles
were merely a distraction and if cuts

and bruises resulted, his rowdy
laugh would convert the most serious

of us and we'd all, for a time, hop
on the wagon; but a life commitment

to fluidity is treacherous: angles
form the contours of our lives

so we have to turn correctly if we're to move;
stop and go's help us maneuver.

Well, at the end, he had to be content
with a rectangular coffin, six

evenly-placed candles and me,
the presider, who now has to extol

in chiseled language and formulaic ritual
a spirit who could never be contained.

Perhaps inviting me for the office
was his last attempt to lure me in.

May angels lead him to Paradise.

THE FONT

This page you're looking at
used to be blank

until a little duck
lost
wandered over it leaving
mud and leaves

then a snake
in consternation
slithered by
leaving goo

and even a hippopotamus
in heavy agitation
stepped on it
leaving unmentionables

but the kicker
was a spry house spider
spreading a silver web
over the whole thing

so it would shine in the dusk
making us think
it was worth
hanging on a wall;

now all can marvel
at the birth of words
and how they grow
into immortality.

ANSEL ADAMS (1902-1984)

All those mountains
with the tonnage of centuries
suddenly leap
    in magic
how you've subverted
gravity to show us
the lightness of creation
a moon stands
    still
with eternal light
aspens stop
    in wonder
and watch you
measuring their fright
you order white
rivers to reflect
our torturous loves
and hold icicles
    in sun -
your own light
has caught the beginning.

SHE STANDS

She struggles along the way
trying to find space
among raucous onlookers

who either crow or weep,
those who have not known;
she remembers wider lanes

and quieter words, a bowl
of wheat and goat's milk
sufficed for a morning spent

with the psalms; prayer the structure
on which a day was slowly built,
a large room for sawing

that spiced the hours and coaxed
the evenings silent; the mystery
of how his feet could run, how his eyes

could slide across a plain and see
wildflowers praise; how he jumped
on her knee eager to learn.

Now she stumbles and climbs
and hears no daily lesson,
but feels etched on her skin

the old prophet's warning.
At noon she is ready and stands
to watch what they will do:

this hill, against a dark sun,
marks the end, and as they lift
the cross, she stands -

she stands - and will not bend
her back for others' sorrow,
will not fail his eyes.

PART VI

THOU HAST MADE ME, AND SHALL THY WORK DECAY?

REPAIR ME NOW, FOR NOW MINE END DOTH HASTE;

I RUN TO DEATH, AND DEATH MEETS ME AS FAST,

AND ALL MY PLEASURES ARE LIKE YESTERDAY.

John Donne, "Thou Hast Made Me"

IF I SHOULD DIE

If I should die before you,
would you make sure my sheets
are clean, my sink is washed

and my hair is combed in its usual
fashion; would you lower the radio's
volume (even Mozart shouldn't intrude),

and delete all messages on my laptop:
treat it as if it, too, has succumbed
to the inevitable and can no longer

receive and send; it will eventually
accept its destiny. Whisper
to my orchid, then bless it. Polish

my doorknobs: I want no fingerprints
left as a residue of my entrances
and exits; shine my shoes

to indicate I've always walked
on the bright side of the street;
and throw my umbrella away:

it was a good companion, but I'd not
want it protecting another's secrets.
Say a prayer, of course; even a mumble

would help; I've mumbled plenty
in my own life and have hoped
I'd be interpreted correctly,

but we don't know, do we?
Try it, anyway, and while you're
kneeling, in shadows and with candles,

recall, if you can, the moments of small
importance, the ones we dismissed -
they have left words that have lingered.

THE TERRIBLE POINT

You never know
where you're going
when you pray:
buses honk
and pages turn,
people run in front
and trip intentions;
it takes time
to pause, reach
into silence, but
once there,
a train takes over
and the terrible point
is you can't direct
the driver, a wizard
who sits dark
behind a hard partition -
not like the movie,
with green smoke
(but with truer magic).
Along the way,
you stop, get out
and walk around the dancers,
watch the fireflies;
a trumpet sounds,
insistent, so you jump

and try the journey again.
No other traveler
for company, just a box
filled with notes and books,
carved animals and canes,
and still they take up
space you want
for other things,
for wondering how
you got aboard,
or how the train winds
its way without a map.

HAMLET: A REVENGE TRAGEDY

You are too damaged
by the crows that surround
your name,
pecking for acorns
they imagine are gold,

so now it's hard to tell
the real gold,
sift the fine words
and with no inky
mist, know you.

There's the tragedy:
a magnificent solitary,
a black cloak
with its back to us.
We should wait.

In another five hundred
years you may emerge
with original power
and lay, once again,
your enemies to rest.

EYESIGHT

He had tried his whole life to see;
he opened closets, soup cans,

books of all kinds, he peered
inside cameras to study lenses

and left the internet exhausted every
morning; impatient and never sure,

he invaded all that was closed;
his eyes hungered to look beyond.

As he walks now, stooped, his eyes
are constrained, their freedom

curtailed; where before they darted
easily across his horizons, leaving

him breathless, they have stilled;
rarely he lifts a heavy head to look,

but through all the years of gazing,
his soul has learned to fashion

its own eyes, so while he walks
or sits in quiet, he smiles, for he sees

now much farther than ever before.

TRANSFIGURATION

I like the daffodils out there:
their long-stemmed insistence
on being first

I like at this time
the small green knobs
pushing against the earth

we know it happens
often, rain clouds
step aside
and bow to a day of light -
but surprise, always,
ice shifts into sun:

farther down than we can go
lies the straining bulb

not a thing to re-plant
but a Word to explode
break into colors
that leap through centuries
of gravel, of wrong turns
to be our yellow umbrellas

this breath that hallows

this gift that splits the old
worn rocks
and flowers in our prayer.

JOLLY GREEN GIANT

They came in all sizes – playfully jostling and cracking
knuckles - from a bearded Lilliputian alcoholic

to a Jolly Green Giant of a woman who cheerfully
wore a bikini; brandishing white banners,

and wearing smiles designed to melt clouds
and make even the largest star collapse in a giggle,

they walked resolutely through the Pearly Gates
and asked a feathered creature to see the Supervisor;

all conversation, hitherto delicately joyous, ceased.
Eyes turned to this rag tag crowd, wondering

what creation had wrought: from what belly of what planet
had come these intruders: had Love really fashioned

what stood before them all? Or had the universe reneged
on its promise of an orderly evolution? They recalled

their own entrance when, to relieve their anxieties,
soft music accompanied the opening of the gates

and ushered them from flesh to spirit, gently,
distracting them from the noise of final rites.

But this crowd needed no distraction: they snapped
their fingers, moved to a raucous rhythm (unblessed?)

and held out fleshly hands to clasp in companionship.
What occurs in the smoke and mirrors of another dimension

is not readily observable, so we cannot say exactly
how the two joined forces, laid plans for wider avenues,

and composed a new music, but the feathered creatures,
it is rumored, stood agog as the Jolly Green Giant bumped

her way down the avenue, passed out scotch and sodas,
and settled back for her daily conversation with the Supervisor.

(For Marge Jonas)

THE WALKER

You offer me a walker, and I suppose
it's time: a necessary nonsense,

to be slighted but used as needed,
and I wonder what else we use

to maneuver; what rigs do we construct
to steer our way? Here I am often,

in the midst of prayer, and I cannot
find a crutch to lead me on to where

I want to go and I wonder if I am
mistaken, if the rig I want is not mine

to find, not mine to hold, but someone else's.

SEASONING

It's all right to sit down quietly
with a plate of pasta on a late afternoon

exchanging smiles and dicey situations
the sun dipping like a slice of bread

in olive oil, shadows eating up
the bolognese; it's all right

to waste your time because
God wastes a whale of years

for us; though God calls it fun-time;
we think to snore is wasteful

but that's because we do not season
our world with love;

so sprinkle around a little more
salt and pepper

and watch it sizzle.

PASSAGE

Each morning
it rises, called for
or not, each

time it's new,
with bright rays
swimming an ocean,

delighting the whales
and dolphins jumping
to catch a glimpse;

then plowing sand
and caressing magnolias
(urging life),

on to vast greens
and browns swaying
in hope (a liturgical

dance to honor
the gods); kissing
the tall rectangles

of cities with quick
flashes, brisk;
on up and over

ice caps
that blush in early
wear, and finally

falling, sated,
on a last west
burnished gold

in thanksgiving.

A FILAMENT OF LOVE

It's like when a soft breeze in the evening
suddenly stops and the sunset glows
its last yellow,

when a gondolier's silent oar turns
to let us off,

when the white gate slips shut
behind us,

when the sparrows, after a day
of darting and foraging, wing their way
back,

when the story line, long labored over,
reaches the final sentence and can breathe,

when the grape is crushed to bring us joy,

when actors retreat as the applause softens,

when the music of Mozart swells before it finds
one note that will carry it, aching, to a finish:

then – the tongue has used its last array
of words and only a desire that chokes
the heart is left, a filament of love
that we trust will light the way.

(For Will and Eldora)

EUCHARIST AT EMMAUS

They should have known because they had
the news, but admittedly the women were excited

and hard to parse so they walked away
and trudge now through the dust like lame cows

feeling sorry for themselves — perhaps regretting
the time spent so far? — but to be kind, also

heartbroken for one they had loved. Events had
swirled around them, a tornado that touched down

and lifted the roofs off all they had built, splintered
the furniture they had assembled, left them

wandering. But — later, they will recall a softer
breeze from behind, a fragrance of life,

and words that cheered like a happy tale will cheer
little children and fill their imagination with

something new, tell their spirits there are reasons,
so they can sit at a meal and discover another

dimension — and more: discover flesh and blood.

EPILOGUE

THESE OLD HANDS

I'm not sure how to begin this —
swallows darting in and around my brain
make my earth a little tipsy —
but I trust that one phrase will catapult me
onto the on-ramp and I'll be in the game.

I happened one day. . . .

and that's how we'll begin. . . .

to look at my hands and found lines
and markings I had not noticed before,

haphazard lines
indicating no one labor or goal

markings of old scars
telling me these hands had fended off
detractors, as if raw battles had been my life

so I searched old letters
newspaper clippings heavy with years
and full of sorry surprises
ran through photographs
(old smiles of old friends).

Not one could testify,
not one could fill in the puzzle,
not one could play the music which would unfold
my memory.

But I will care for them, these old hands
that know more than I do and so need
a daily blessing

these old hands that lift and grasp and caress
and point the way, unerringly. . . .

and that's how we'll end.

ACKNOWLEDGMENTS

The following poems, included in this volume, have been previously published; some of them have undergone slight changes since their initial publication.

Kansas Quarterly: "The Orphan Bear," "Good Taste," "A Formic Study"
Negative Capability: "Poppies"
The Owl: "Since You Know"
Santa Clara Review: "The Maker"
Studies in Jesuit Spirituality: "The Walker"
Sacred Journey: "Transfiguration"
The Penwood Review: "The Terrible Point"
Jesuit Province of California Website: "The Old Chair"
Mississippi Valley Review: "Primitivism"
The CEA Critic: "Le Morte d'Arthur"
The Vineyard: "Seasoning," "Roly-Poly"
DeKalb Literary Arts Journal: "Roses"

My grateful thanks to James Torrens, S.J., for his usual astute, careful and helpful criticism, and to Michael Zampelli, S.J., and the Jesuit Community of Santa Clara University, for their daily support.

14603183R00077

Made in the USA
San Bernardino, CA
30 August 2014